MARCHING FOR FAUSA

To Stephen Jeffreys and Peter Thomson

'BIYI BANDELE

MARCHING FOR FAUSA

AMBER LANE PRESS

All rights whatsoever in this play are strictly reserved and application for performance, etc. must be made before rehearsals begin to:
MBA Literary Agents Ltd
45 Fitzroy Street
London W1P 5HR

No performance may be given unless a licence has been obtained.

First published in 1993 by
Amber Lane Press Ltd
Cheorl House
Church Street
Charlbury
Oxford OX7 3PR
Telephone: 0608 810024

Printed in Great Britain by
Bocardo Press Ltd, Didcot, Oxon

Copyright © 'Biyi Bandele, 1993

The right of 'Biyi Bandele to be identified as author of this work has been asserted by him in accordance with Section 77 of the Copyright, Designs and Patents Act 1988.

ISBN 1 872868 10 X

CONDITIONS OF SALE
This book is sold subject to the condition that it shall not, by way of trade or otherwise, be lent, re-sold, hired out or otherwise circulated without the publisher's prior consent in any form of binding or cover other than that in which it is published and without a similar condition including this condition being imposed on the subsequent purchaser.

CHARACTERS

TELANI BALARABE
a journalist and photographer

DR OLATIDE KIRIYO
Honourable Minister of Cultural Affairs

TALATA MAI NONO
Kiriyo's Personal Assistant

NNEKA ALAKIJA-BROWN
Editor of the NewsDay-on-Sunday

ZAK ZEBRUDAYA
Features Editor of the NewsDay-on-Sunday

EBENEZER MANCHOK   TIMO
NEHUSTA   MODUPE LABARI
Students

TWO STATE SECURITY OFFICERS

BUSINESSMAN

SCHOOLTEACHER

POLICE OFFICERS

ARMY OFFICERS

DELEGATION OF WOMEN

Marching for Fausa was first given a rehearsed reading (under the title *Telani's Graffiti*) at the Royal Court Theatre Upstairs, London, on 25th June 1992. It was directed by Annie Castledine with the following cast:

TELANI	Taiwo Payne
KIRIYO	Patrice Naiambana
TALATA	Bola Aiyeola
EBENEZER	Dhobei Operai
NNEKA	Pauline Black
ZAK	Leo Wringer
SSS 1	Dhobei Operai
SCHOOLTEACHER	Patrice Naiambana
BUSINESSMAN	Dhobei Operai
ARMY OFFICER 1	Dhobei Operai
ARMY OFFICER 2	Leo Wringer
'ALLELUIA' POLICE OFFICER	Leo Wringer
LEADER OF THE WOMEN	Bola Aiyeola

The play was subsequently presented at the Royal Court Theatre Upstairs, London, on 13th January 1993. It was directed by Annie Castledine with the following cast:

TELANI	Susan Aderin
KIRIYO	Patrice Naiambana
TALATA	Pamela Nomvete
EBENEZER	Femi Elufowoju
NNEKA	Pauline Black
ZAK	Leo Wringer
SSS 1	Jude Akuwudike
SCHOOLTEACHER	Patrice Naiambana
BUSINESSMAN	Femi Elufowoju
ARMY OFFICER 1	Jude Akuwudike
ARMY OFFICER 2	Leo Wringer
'ALLELUIA' POLICE OFFICER	Leo Wringer
LEADER OF THE WOMEN	Pamela Nomvete

All other parts played by members of the company.

Designer Martin Johns
Lighting Jon Linstrum
Music by Juwon Ogungbe

Once, for a dare,
He filled his heart-shaped swimming pool
With banknotes, high denomination
And fed a pound of caviar to his dog.
The dog was sick; a chartered plane
Flew in replacement for the Persian rug.

— Wole Soyinka

In my first hours in Phnom Penh I took no photographs;
incredulity saw to that.

— John Pilger

Note: This script went to press before rehearsals of *Marching for Fausa*. Some alterations may therefore have been made during the production process.

ACT ONE

Cell ten at the Special Interrogations Centre, State Security Service on an island on the outskirts of Songi, capital city of the Federal Republic of Songhai.

In the darkness we see a figure slouched over in a chair, head hung down by the side as if detached from the body and hanging from a string.

Also in the darkness we hear a man's voice, in recitation, coming from neighbouring Cell nine.

VOICE: [*off*] My dear brodas an' sistas, I say good mor'ing to you all. Dis medicine which I hold for hand so is what we call endometacin capsule, otherwise known as endocin capsule.
 [*Silence.*]
 [*Heavy footfalls. A jangling of keys against metal. Footfalls. The voice from Cell nine is heard again.*]
 [*off*] Endometacin capsule is good for you.
 Is good for man an' woman.
 Is good for child an' good for children.
 Endometacin capsule will cure *anything*.
 Na headache de worry you?
 Take two tablets an' 'e go vanish.
 Na your prick refuse to perform?
 Endometacin will resurrect it.
 Na your teeth dirty like Agege motorway?
 Endometacin is di dental detergent.
 [*A passionate rush of angry, pleading, protesting voices swallows the rest of this gibberish. Absolute silence.*]
 [*The voice of* SSS 1 *is heard.*]
SSS 1: [*off*] Three, two, one.
 [*Rapid gunfire.*]

[*Darkness still on stage. The seated figure remains slumped.*]

[*A radio is switched on.*]

RADIO: The cost in financial terms of the riots — the worst this country has witnessed in over three decades — is yet to be officially estimated. Analysts are in no doubt that it will run into the hundreds of millions . . .

Lights come on to reveal a besuited State Security Officer, whom we shall hereafter know as SSS 1, *reaching for a knob and switching off the radio. It is on a small desk beside the seated figure. With his other hand* SSS 1 *reaches for the head of the slumped figure and swings it upright. Lights should be focused on the woman in the chair who now struggles to open her eyes in the face of powerful lights that have been trained on her. Her name is* TELANI BALARABE. *She is in her late twenties or early thirties. Throughout this scene the lights will be riveted on her. Although we shall see very clearly* SSS 1 *and his subordinate,* SSS 2, *they should be endowed with an aura of almost clinical facelessness.*

SSS 1: So there.

SSS 2: Sheer idiocy, Madam Balarabe. Idiocy. With big 'E'.

[*Pause.*]

[*Footfalls along the corridor. Two rapid gunshots.*]

[SSS 1 *cracks his knuckles. Then, in a voice that is neither friendly nor hostile or gloating, he addresses* TELANI.]

SSS 1: Rufus Swung His Face At Last To The Wind Then His Neck Snapped.

ACT ONE 11

SSS 2: [*lost*] I beg your pudding, sir. Which one be Rufus?
SSS 1: Relax, Officer. We are approaching territories out of your depth here. We're delving into matters of acquired taste. Music, if you must know. Classical. Jazz.
[*He lifts up* TELANI's *head.*]
Surely you shan't let me down?
TELANI: Take your hands off me. [*wearily*] Archie Shepp.
[SSS 1 *turns triumphantly to* SSS 2.]
SSS 1: There. You'll do well to pay heed to Miss Balarabe. She's cultured. That is why she knows that Rufus Swung His Face At Last To The Wind Then His Neck Snapped is not the name of a detainee, but the title of a song. [*Pause.*] That is not to say that we might not have — in any one of these ten cells on this corridor — some gentleman by the name of Rufus. If there is — and I doubt that there is — he should be happy to be informed that he wasn't among the three executed just now.
[*He pulls out a sheet from a file* SSS 2 *is carrying and consults it.*]
Of that he can be certain. He's not dead. And when the time does come, which it will undoubtedly, Officer, he'll be despatched by the most humane means possible. We're not in the habit of hanging people here. Do you understand?
SSS 2: [*with a petrified salute*] Yes, sir.
SSS 1: [*to* TELANI] Three down. Seven to go. We have a high respect for numbers, Miss Balarabe. That's why we're doing this — numerically. Your friends in Cells one, two and three had to be the first to go. In that order. It was my unhappy responsibility to oversee the executions of the

first two. And I went to great lengths to assure them that it was nothing personal. If they'd been in Cells eight, nine and ten rather than one, two and three who am I to begrudge them of those precious extra hours of relishing the air of this world and the goodness thereof? Personally, I wouldn't miss the air around here. Toxic waste, automobile exhaust, pyramids of garbage — and simple flatulence. Still.

> [*He tosses a cigarette at her. It rolls to a stop beside the radio. She does not touch it. He lights one himself.*]

Still, that is not to say that you're not lucky, Miss Balarabe. You're in Cell number ten, after all.

> [*He picks up the cigarette, lights it from his own and inserts it between her lips. She still does not touch it. It burns away.*]

Obviously you'll realise that sooner or later the footfalls will come thundering down that corridor, keys inserted in the lock, and when that door opens it shan't be myself, or Officer here, come to offer you a cigarette. You'll appreciate that we are running out of space; there are dozens of other suspects we have to interrogate and, most importantly, His Excellency wants this business dealt with ASAP.

> [*Simultaneously with the above the voice from Cell nine is heard.*]

VOICE: [*off*] Endometacin will cure rashes, boils, eczema, dandruff, malaria, hay fever, rabies, syphilis, gonorrhoea, even AIDS self. Na kia-kia bus. Onitsha-by-Air. No speed limit for heaven. You want am sista? Broda me? Only two naira for one sachet, kia-kia bus, no speed limit for heaven.

SSS 1: That gorilla in Cell nine, for instance: the only reason he's still in a position to be noising himself on our consciences is because of this numbers thing, i.e. he's in number nine, and we haven't got there yet.

[TELANI *is smoking her cigarette for the first time — her first real sign of animation. Her voice is hoarse, a harsh whisper.*]

TELANI: Who is he?

SSS 1: In trying to make him cooperate, some of my more zealous colleagues were forced to subject the poor wretch to a series of rather experimental methods of persuasion, one of which involved the application of electric shocks to his mental faculties. Unfortunately their only guide was a highly complicated, not to say dubious, DIY booklet which purports to teach these things to the Absolute Beginner. Absolute hogwash, more like. They ended up leaving him with neither one nor the other: a split personality. Spilt. So that one moment he's quiet as can be, the next he's an itinerant quack chemist. He's become a vegetable; of no conceivable use to us — or indeed to himself. The sooner he goes the better for all concerned.

[*He bends down as if to whisper in her ear.*]

Do you want to end up like that thing? All we're asking you to do, Telani — do you mind if I call you Telani? — is *confirm* certain things. We're not asking you to name names, we're not asking you to give us information, we're certainly not asking you to grass on anybody. All we ask of you, Telani — look at me — I don't take any pleasure from doing this, the fact is, someone has to do it and that person . . . At the end of every month I go to the pay office like every other civil servant. I tender my pay voucher, quibble over tax deductions, make sure extra hours, such as these, have been taken into consideration; I take my family out to the beach, arm-wrestle with the kids, watch the nine o'clock news, make love to my wife — and I've never cheated on her. And like most car-owners these days, jump-start the car every morning. I go to church as well, Miss Balarabe. In my line of job there's no such thing as a personal vendetta. Personally, I have nothing against you. Any anger, any use of persuasive aggression — if I should lose my head — figurative — and blow yours off — literal — it would be purely and sincerely an act of duty — joke. So, Telani . . . [*He is now shouting although he does not seem to realise it.*] . . . for the tenth time, do you recognise any of these names?

[*He slaps the cigarette out of her hand and stamps on it. He pulls out another sheet from* SSS 2*'s file and thrusts it into her face.*]

TELANI: [*without looking at the paper*] No.
SSS 1: No?
TELANI: No.

[SSS 1*'s wristwatch gives off a series of bleeps. He checks the time.*]

SSS 1: I'm afraid it's time for another one. I shall be back with you shortly.

[*He snatches the file from* SSS 2 *and marches out.*]
[*Pause.*]

TELANI: [*quietly*] Time for another what?

[*A shot rings out.*]

SSS 2: [*subdued*] There's timetable, Madam Balarabe. At least one must go every forty-five minutes or so. Why are you so strong-headed, for God's sake? Why can't you just say yes, yes, yes, I know that one, I don't recognise these, I remember those . . . ? Why can't you fit do the logical thing and walk out of here or at least get a reprieve, your sentence commuted?

TELANI: I haven't been tried. Have I been sentenced already?

SSS 2: Come on, Madam Balarabe, this is treason we're talking of, not a traffic offence. Don't let's waste our time.

TELANI: I do not know any of these names.

[*She steps forward and addresses the audience.*]

About Songhai, there really isn't much to tell. It's a populous country on the west coast of Africa, shares many town names with Nigeria, its nearest neighbour to the west, and with whom it once shared colonial masters. They continue to share a common currency. Many Songhaians prefer to describe Songhai not as a country but as an artificial welding together of nations who, if they'd had a say in the matter, would actually *emigrate* in order to avoid each other. At the last count there were four hundred linguistic groups in the country. Too many cooks, some say, that's why nothing ever turned out to be what it seemed.

My story begins in a classroom in a seedy little high school in downtown Songi, the nation's capital city. I wasn't there that morning but . . . [*shrugs*] . . . It all began with the palaver over a sixteen-year-old girl called Fausatu.

[*She steps back to the interrogation chair, completely back in character.*]

SSS 2: Madam Balarabe, are you very sure say you no know any of dis names at all? At all? Because if you know am 'e go better make you talk now.

Dis na your opportunity. And you self know say opportunity once lost can never be regain.

[TELANI *stares at the sheet for a long while.*]

TELANI: I do not know any of these names.

We commence on a journey through TELANI's *mind. It begins with a classroom in an Ajegunle school.*

TEACHER: Ebenezer Manchok.
EBENEZER: Presen' sah.
TEACHER: Modupe Labari.
MODUPE: Presen' sah.
TEACHER: Timo Solomon.
TIMO: Presen' sah.
TEACHER: Fausa Ibrahima.
EBENEZER: She never come, sah.

[*In his almost mechanical haste the* TEACHER *has gone on to the next name before realising that the last response wasn't from the student whose name he had called.*]

TEACHER: Nehusta Fazi —
NEHUSTA: Presen' sah.
TEACHER: No . . . Wait a minute . . . Who answered just now when I called out Fausa's name?
EBENEZER: I sah.

[*The* TEACHER *tilts his glasses to the tip of his nose, a sign of fury.*]

TEACHER: What did you say? Ebenezer Manchok.

[*As the boy is about to respond an uproar from the next class drowns out his voice. The* TEACHER *storms to the cardboard wall which partitions the classes.*]

Miss Lawal, I shall not repeat this one more time: if you cannot control your students go back home and face your knitting.

[*The noise continues unabated.*]
This is no joking matter, Miss Lawal. If you can't handle those thugs in your class please kindly rid us of them. Donate them to the zoo. At least they'd cease to be a nuisance. We might even pay for the privilege of going to see them. Please, Miss Lawal, please.
[*The noise worsens. A volley of paper balls assails the* TEACHER's *head. He goes back to his seat mouthing expletives.*]
Yes, Ebenezer, you were saying?
EBENEZER: [*tittering*] I say di girl de come, sah.
TEACHER: [*infinitely patient*] I take it by that you mean Fausa is not present in class this morning and you know the reason why.
EBENEZER: Hundred over hundred, sah.
TEACHER: Beg your —
EBENEZER: Da's right, sah. Di girl de come.
TEACHER: [*leans forward*] Can you do us one tiny favour, please?
EBENEZER: [*expectantly*] Sah?
TEACHER: Speak English. This is a classroom, Ebenezer. Not Iddo Motor-Park.
EBENEZER: Yes, sah.
TEACHER: Good. Now, could you tell us once more what you've just said about Miss Ibrahima?
EBENEZER: I say di girl de come.
TEACHER: In English, Mr Manchok, tell us in English.
EBENEZER: [*infinitely patient*] I speaking English, Tisha Kakaki. I say di girl de come. Whish language be dat: Frensh?
[*The class begins to giggle.*]
TEACHER: [*with an effort*] Queen's English, Mr Manchok, *proper* English.
[*A puzzled silence in class.*]
EBENEZER: Queen's English, sah?

[He clears his throat, holds his nose and anglicises his delivery.]

Di girl de cooome, saaah.

TEACHER: [fully exasperated] Mr Manchok!

EBENEZER: [innocently] Sah? I say Fausa will be come to school after Moses has part the Red Sea with his rod.

TEACHER: After Moses has parted the Red Sea with his rod? I'm afraid I fail to get your meaning, Mr Manchok.

EBENEZER: It's Fausa's wedding today, Teacher Kakaki.

TIMO: Wedding for *where*? She's being given away today, is what's happening, not a bloody wedding.

NEHUSTA: Same thing. At end of the day the same thing happens. Moses will part the Red Sea with his . . .

[She makes a suggestive gesture.]

TEACHER: Moses who?

MODUPE: That is the word of God you debase, you lot. I fear for your souls.

ALL: [simultaneously] Forgive us, oh Lord, for we have sinned.

[They stick out their tongues at MODUPE.]

TEACHER: Can anyone tell me what's going on in this class? Who is Moses?

TIMO: Man died over four thousand years ago, sir. Great-grand-uncle of Jesus Christ. *He* lived over two thousand years ago.

TEACHER: What on earth has come over you this morning?

EBENEZER: The Moses in question here is a man called Halilu. Tonight he liberates Fausa from the bondage of virginity.

TIMO: Not that she was one, to begin with.

EBENEZER: And how do you know that, Mr Peacock?

TIMO: The earth speaks to me, brother, I pee on it and seeds become roots. The earth is mine and I am

the earth's. I water the earth, brother, and feed
from its wealth.
MODUPE: Bollocks.
EBENEZER: Sir, there goes a rider who mounts horses in
daylight and human beings at night.
NEHUSTA: A dejected lover.
MODUPE: A miserable wretch.
TIMO: Misery is my sky tonight. When you count my
stars one shall be missing. But as our fathers
say —
MODUPE: Not to mention our mothers who actually said
it.
EBENEZER: May your road be rough.
NEHUSTA: And your path a bed of spikes.
TIMO: So that the soles of your feet are hardened.
EBENEZER: Against the thorns of this world.
TEACHER: Huinh?
EBENEZER: Fausa's hand is being given in marriage today,
Teacher Kakaki.
TEACHER: I understand that — I mean, I don't really —
but what has that got to do with this — this
lunacy?
 [*A sudden commotion across the wall completes the* TEACHER's *disorientation. It is the voices of the pupils in Miss Lawal's class insistently raised in song.*]
VOICES 1: All we are saying:
Give us Fausa.
VOICES 2: Halilu se'ologbo ni
Wa'a sare
Halilu se'ologbo ni
Wa'a sare gidi   [*etc, etc, intermittently*]
TEACHER: Will someone please tell me what is
happening . . . ?
EBENEZER: It's a forced marriage, is what we're saying.
Fausa hardly knew this fellow, this Halilu person she's being given away to tonight.

NEHUSTA: In fact, until two days ago she'd never met him.
MODUPE: It had been arranged a long time ago.
TIMO: Long before Fausa was born —
EBENEZER: That this man, a friend of her father's, would marry the child if it was a girl.
MODUPE: It was a marriage made in heaven.
NEHUSTA: Fausa managed to get a note to us. Help.
MODUPE: She wanted help.
NEHUSTA: So we had a meeting last night. [*pointedly*] Us girls, that is. At the hostel.
EBENEZER: We too, they hadn't a clue we knew what was going down. We had our own meeting.
NEHUSTA: At *our* meeting, which lasted the better part of the night, we decided to go on a march today.
EBENEZER: As it happened, we'd come to the same decision. We met them this morning during assembly and, through the kind offices of Fausa's boyfriend, Timo here . . .
MODUPE: Who, despite his hinted claims to the contrary, had not even peeled the yam, not to talk of eating it —
EBENEZER: We decided to act together. And so, Tisha Kakaki, this morning na school — free. We are —
ALL: [*as if on cue*] Marching for Fausa.

[*They pull out placards from underneath their lockers. Inscriptions range from FREE FAUSA to MARRIAGES ARE NOT MADE IN HEAVEN. They join the other class in song.*]

[*The* TEACHER *runs to peep over the wall.*]

TEACHER: Miss Lawal, Miss Lawal, what shall we do about this madness . . . ?

[*In response, a placard is thrown at him from across the wall. It reads: FREE FAUSA.*]

Oh no, Miss Lawal, surely not you too . . .

[*The* STUDENTS *descend on him, playfully*

knocking him around, until he joins in the singing. As they achieve this there is an outburst of machine-gun fire offstage. All freeze. Silence. EBENEZER *cautiously makes his way to a window.*]

EBENEZER: [*peeping out*] Kutuman babban burau Uban nan.

[*He ducks a stray bullet, whistles then swears. He turns to the class.*]

It's the zombies.

TEACHER: [*from beneath a desk*] Zombies?

EBENEZER: [*solemnly*] Fucking zombies, sir.

TEACHER: This is no time for gutter language, Ebenezer, hardly time for flippancy.

[*A loud explosion, followed by dazzling fireworks, casts the classroom into darkness.*]

Lights come on again to reveal an ARMY OFFICER *behind a studio microphone in a radio station. He is flanked on both sides by grim-looking bodyguards.*

TELANI *enters in her working gear: a pair of overalls and a baggage of cameras.*

TELANI: My father used to describe himself — he's retired now — as a real-estate agent. In actual fact in Songi there's an entire street named after him. It seemed only fair, seeing as he owned all the houses on it.

Like many from his generation he had seen his way through school and college by chopping trees for firewood. They started their business — him and my mum — in the fifties, having trained as lawyers. He was a politician then — or, as they came to be known in our history books — a nationalist. He belonged to a group of brash, highly articulate, zealously anti-imperialist young men and women.

They assumed that they — being eminently fit and able — should by right inherit the baton of power from the departing representatives of 'Queen and Country'. On the other hand, the Colonial Officers considered them — and probably rightly, too — generally haughty, disdainful and "Not the sort of fellows one would like to do business with". Obviously, it was essential that those to whom they would bequeath the reins of government should be "Fellows they could do business with".

There wasn't a shortage of such people. They existed, in abundance.

There was also the army. At that time in Songhai no parent would openly admit that their son had joined the army. It was regarded as the garbage heap of ambition. The received wisdom was that the future belonged to the professionals: doctors, lawyers, accountants. The bulk of the army was made up of dropouts, the dregs of society, those who had not the means — and, sometimes, not the inclination — to pursue what was then known as the golden fleece. The best of these were later sent to Sandhurst in England to train to be officers. They, and not the arrogant professionals, stepped into the shoes that the colonialists left.

By the time people like my parents woke up to the fact that one gun was mightier than a thousand university degrees the soldiers had, as it were, brought the circus to town. They'd already infected the country with a fastly addictive game of cowboys-and-robbers known as 'The Coup'.

[TELANI *leaves.*]

OFFICER: In the name of the Supreme Council of the Revolution of the Songhaian armed forces I declare martial law over the Federal Republic of Songhai. The constitution is suspended and the regional governments and elected assemblies are hereby dissolved. All political, cultural, tribal and trade union activities, together with all demonstrations and unauthorised gatherings, are banned until further notice.

The aim of the Revolutionary Council is to establish a strong, united and prosperous nation, free from corruption and internal strife. Our methods of achieving this are strictly military but we have no doubt that every Songhaian will give us maximum cooperation by assisting the regime and not, repeat not, disturbing the peace during the slight changes that are taking place.

This is not, repeat not, a time for long speech-making and so let me acquaint you with ten proclamations in the Extraordinary Orders of the Day which the Supreme Council has promulgated. These will be modified as the situation improves.

>[*Enter a mud-splattered figure, out of breath and obviously glad to be inside. It is* TELANI. *She has an assortment of cameras and camera equipment hanging from her shoulders. She sets up her camera equipment while the bodyguards frisk her. She seems to be used to being searched and her whole attention appears to be on setting up her camera. She positions herself.*]

>[*The* ARMY OFFICER *continues his broadcast.*]

Number One: You are hereby warned that looting, rape, embezzlement, bribery or corruption, obstruction of the revolution, sabotage, subversion, false alarm and assistance of foreign invaders are all offences punishable by death sentence.

[TELANI *snaps.*]

Number Two: Demonstrations, unauthorised assembly, non-cooperation with the revolutionary troops are punishable in the very manner of death.

[*The* ARMY OFFICER *notices* TELANI. *She snaps.*]

Number Three: Assistance to persons attempting to escape justice and failure to report anti-revolution activities are punishable in the very manner of death.

[*He makes the motions of striking a pose.* TELANI *snaps.*]

Number Four: Refusal or neglect to perform any duty or any task that may of necessity be ordered by local military commanders in support of the change will be punished by death sentence.

[*He strikes a pose. Snap, snap.*]

Number Five: Spying, harmful or injurious publications, and broadcasts of troop movements or actions will be punished by death sentence.

[*He strikes another pose. Snap, snap.*]

Number Six: Shouting of slogans, loitering, rowdy behaviour will be rectified by any sentence of severe castration — beg your pardon — incarceration or death sentence.

[*Snap, snap, snap.*]

Number Seven: Doubtful loyalty will be penalised by imprisonment or any more severe punishment sentence.

[*Poses. Snap, snap, snap.*]

Number Eight: Illegal possession or carrying of firearms, arms smuggling, or attempts to escape with documents, valuables, including money or other assets vital to the running of any establishment, will be punished by death sentence.

[*Different poses. Snap, snap, snap.*]

Number Nine: Wavering or sitting on the fence and failing to declare open loyalty for the revolution will be regarded as an act of hostility punishable by any sentence deemed suitable.

[*Snap, snap, snap.*]

Number Ten: Tearing down of an order of the day or proclamation or any other authorised notices will be penalised by death sentence.

[*Snap, snap, snap.*]

My dear countrymen — and women — no citizen should have any fear.

[*Snap, snap, snap.*]

Our enemies are the political profiteers, swindlers, the men in high and low places that seek bribes and demand ten percent, those that seek to keep this country divided permanently so that they can remain in office as ministers and VIPs of waste —

[*A loud explosion announces the arrival of a new wave of soldiers into the studio. Darkness as the power supply is short-circuited.*]

A few seconds later: lights flood back in as windows are opened to let out smoke.

The bodies of the ARMY OFFICER *and his men are unceremoniously dragged out of the studio. A new* ARMY OFFICER *takes over the microphone.*

Meanwhile TELANI *is engaged in a heated exchange with the new bodyguards.*

OFFICER 2: [*into the microphone*] Fellow compatriots: there has been a change of government. Nothing to do with the twaddle that revolutionary nit was blabbing over the airwaves a few moments ago.

TELANI: [*in the background*] I told you already, I'm a journalist —

OFFICER 2: [*into the microphone*] As a matter of fact . . .

[*The full import of what their leader is doing hits the* LIEUTENANTS. *They let go of* TELANI *and step forward.*]

LIEUTENANT: [*loud whisper*] Read the speech.

OFFICER 2: What?

LIEUTENANT: The speech, sir, the speech. With all due respect, sir, this is no breakfast show. You can't go on chatting like that, it isn't — military. [*beckons to a colleague*] Tell the engineer to stop broadcasting for a minute . . .

OFFICER 2: What in heaven's name are you talking about, what speech — ?

[TELANI, *who has been setting up her scattered equipment all this while, now spots on the floor some blood-stained, crumpled sheets of paper. She picks them up and hands them to the* LIEUTENANT *with a placatory 'Will this help?' expression. The* LIEUTENANT *hastily gathers the papers together, re-arranges them and scans them. He shoves the lot into* OFFICER 2's *hands.*]

LIEUTENANT: There's your speech, sir. There must always be a speech. Right, engineers, one, two —

OFFICER 2: In the name of the Supreme Council of the Revolution of the Songhaian armed forces I declare martial law over the Federal Republic of Songhai. The constitution is suspended and the regional governments and elected assemblies are hereby dissolved —

[TELANI *is poised with her camera and silently, but with exaggerated gestures, mouthing the word 'Frown' to* OFFICER 2. *He returns with a blank and irritated stare.*]

TELANI: [*loud whisper and louder gestures*] Frown, sir, for the camera!

> [OFFICER 2 *now understands and obliges with a photogenic smile.* TELANI *contorts her face to get her meaning across. Now he gets it.*]
> [*As* TELANI *takes a series of snaps, we see, through a sequence of slide-shots,* OFFICER 2 *in a variety of frowns.*]

> *We segue into the office of* HIS EXCELLENCY DR OLATIDE KIRIYO, *Honourable Minister of Cultural Affairs. Directly above his head is a portrait of* OFFICER 2, *now Head-of-State, resplendent in uniform. It is from the set taken at the radio station.*
> TALATA, KIRIYO's *secretary, enters.*

TALATA: Do you have a minute to spare, sir? The progress report to His Excellency the Head-of-State is due tomorrow.

KIRIYO: Is it? Which report, if I may so ask, and why are you only now telling me?

TALATA: On our preparations for the National Women's Day, Your Excellency. And I've been reminding you for the past week. Another thing, sir, there's a lady in the reception waiting to see you. A reporter from the *NewsDay*.

> [TALATA *hands him a card.*]

KIRIYO: [*reading from the card*] Telani Balarabe. [*repeats it to himself*] Oh — that Telani Balarabe? That one who goes about harassing innocent ministers with cameras? The columnist?

TALATA: Yes, Your Excellency —

KIRIYO: [*shaking his head*] Regrets, regrets, regrets.

TALATA: Actually, sir, she says it's pertaining to the Women's Day.

KIRIYO: Is it? Tell her to come back tomorrow. Which

reminds me, I need to speak to the editor of the *NewsDay* at some point this morning.

[*He seems to notice* TALATA *for the first time.*] I wonder what's happened to my manners this morning. Have I complimented your exquisite choice of dress today? Not that on any other day you've been lacking in that department. You look — shall we say — ravishing in that outfit.

TALATA: Thank you, sir. A birthday gift from my boyfriend.

KIRIYO: Your boyfriend? Quite, quite. I see. Now, to this progress report.

TALATA: I'm ready when you are.

KIRIYO: Promises, promises. Now then, how shall we start? Yes, oh yes . . . What was the subject?

TALATA: A progress report on your preparations for the oncoming National Women's Day, Your Excellency.

KIRIYO: Yes, of course Talata, of course. My memory. Not what it used to be.

TALATA: [*calmly*] You were about to begin the progress report.

KIRIYO: Yes, progress report. Here we go: to His Excellency, the Head-of-State, Commander-in-Chief of the Armed Forces, Major General Salu Bata Marimasha —

TALATA: His Excellency, the Head-of-State, Commander-in-Chief of the Armed Forces, Major General Salu Bata Marimasha . . .

KIRIYO: [*settling back comfortably*] Your Excellency, it is with great joy, great great joy, that I address this report to your august office. How fares the First Lady . . . ? And the children? Mine are alright. Wives and children, I mean to say. And growing up, at an alarmingly fast rate . . . As to our preparations for the Women's Day, I must say, Your Excellency, that plans are going according to schedule. No hitches whatsoever. The fashion pageant is in hand, some of our most beautiful women in the land, I assure you. And some really ecstatic dancers too. In addition to that — oh yes, Your Excellency, there's more — in addition to that we shall be having a session on the True African Woman: *Who is the True African Woman?* We've got a panel of ten learned men of letters, selected from the cream of the chattering classes, to trash this very interesting topic. Finally, Your Excellency, without any intention of chest-beating, I must say be there, it promises to be the most successful National Women's Day this country has seen.

TALATA: Most successful . . . this country has seen . . . Is that all, sir?

KIRIYO: For now, yes. Now, just a matter of interest . . .

TALATA: Yes?

KIRIYO: This boyfriend of yours —

TALATA: Sir?

KIRIYO: Does he work around here?

TALATA: Why, sir?

KIRIYO: Maybe . . . he needs a — transfer?

TALATA: I don't think so, Your Excellency.

KIRIYO: Very well. Could you get me the contracts file, please? Tenders and bidders.

[TALATA *begins to leave.*]

TALATA: Rightio. I won't be a moment.

KIRIYO: Miss Mai Nono?

TALATA: [*pausing by the door*] Sir?

KIRIYO: Be a darling, get me Mrs Alakija-Brown of the *NewsDay* on the line, please.

TALATA: Of course, Your Excellency.

As TALATA *exits the Minister's office is instantaneously transformed into the Editorial Suite of the NewsDay-on-Sunday, where we walk into an editorial meeting consisting of the paper's editor,* NNEKA ALAKIJA-BROWN, *a middle-aged woman of a stern, sometimes matronly countenance;* TELANI; *and a seemingly toady of a man called* ZAK ZEBRUDAYA, *the features editor. His guile is slick and shameless. There is the incessant noise of clattering typewriters in the background: the hum of the newsroom. Also the sound of a radio tuned in to a news station.*

NNEKA: And the lead stories, has anyone given a thought to that?
TELANI: I've done a story on the Ajegunle children —
NNEKA: The Ajegunle children?
TELANI: A group of schoolkids in Ajegunle who are staging a protest on behalf of a mate of theirs who has been sold into marriage —
NNEKA: You've lost me, I'm afraid —
TELANI: A forced marriage, Mrs Editor, a throw-back to marriage-by-post.
NNEKA: Interesting. But — why would anyone wish to buy a paper that lectures them on marriage-by-post?
TELANI: This is a bit different, Ma — for several good reasons: firstly, this girl, Fausa, was actually given away *before* she was born. Second, she's barely sixteen. Third, these are the nineties not the forties. Fourth, there happens to be now a law against that sort of thing.
NNEKA: A law? [*laughs*] There's also a bigamy law in case you don't know. Never been a conviction under it. Why? Because every second man in the land will be in gaol if it came to that. That's no front page material, I'm afraid, Miss

Balarabe. What do you think, Mr Features?
ZAK: Madam? Oh, yes, absolutely with you, Ma. I agree with you. Absolutely.

[NNEKA *flips through the dummy pages in front of her.*]

NNEKA: Beneath classified ads or at the foot of Lonely Hearts. No? Two columns under obituaries?
TELANI: Obituaries, Madam Editor? Actually, these kids are very much alive —
NNEKA: Not for much longer, if they take to the streets, I tell you. [*a conciliatory look*] Surely you don't need to be told our position on these things?
TELANI: I know, Mrs Alakija-Brown. It's just that — they're only kids. What harm can they do?
NNEKA: You'd be surprised. In the meantime, I've got a rather important assignment for you —
TELANI: I thought we were still on to the Front Page —
NNEKA: Yes, weren't we. Which brings me to the grievous printer's error in last week's Front Page.
TELANI: I was going to ask about that, what was it? I don't seem to remember noticing any.

[NNEKA *passes her a copy of the newspaper.*]

NNEKA: Spotted it? No?

[TELANI *still does not find the error.* NNEKA *takes the paper back from her.*]

There you have it. The caption under the Head-of-State's picture.
TELANI: [*reads*] "His Excellency, the Head-of-State, Major General Salu Bata Marimasha . . ." [*looks up, puzzled*] What's wrong with that?

[NNEKA *smiles knowingly at* ZAK.]

NNEKA: Tell her.
ZAK: Something has been erroneously omitted there. The full and correct title of His Excellency, the Head-of-State, *Commander-in-Chief of the Armed Forces*, Major General Salu Bata Marimasha is His Excellency, the Head-of-State,

Commander-in-Chief of the Armed Forces, Major General Salu Bata Marimasha.

TELANI: [*incredulous*] That is the grievous error — the omission of 'Commander-in-Chief of the Armed Forces'?

NNEKA: [*nods gravely*] The front page shall be devoted to our unconditional apology to His Excellency for any embarrassment this might have caused him. By the way, he thought those were very nice photographs of him you took at the radio station on the day of the take-over.

[TELANI *responds to the first half of* NNEKA's *speech.*]

TELANI: I see.

NNEKA: [*to* TELANI] You've got to realise that there are some who have been going around slandering His Excellency, claiming that all he's been doing since he came into power is promote himself.

ZAK: But it's true, isn't it?

[*He catches himself just in time and quickly goes on.*]

But then, what's wrong with that? There's no law after all that prevents a Head-of-State from promoting himself.

[*He throws worried looks in* NNEKA's *direction.*]

NNEKA: [*pointedly ignoring him*] It would not be in the interest of the *NewsDay* for us to be seen as begrudging His Excellency of his true rank and position. [*now turns to him*] Otherwise we just might not be here much longer to cause any further embarrassments.

TELANI: I see. You mentioned an assignment.

NNEKA: Yes. An interview with the Minister of Culture on this forthcoming National Women's Day.

TELANI: I'm already on to that.

NNEKA: Are you?

TELANI: I've made an appointment to see the Minister.

NNEKA: Good. Good. We need it for a profile we're running next week.

> [*She glances at her watch and immediately springs up.*]

I'm afraid I must dash this very minute or I'm going to be late for an exclusive with the Education Minister. Good Day. [*behind her shoulder*] Keep up the good work, Miss Balarabe. It shan't go unrewarded. And remember — this is nothing personal. We're all only doing our jobs —

> [*The radio has been turned up so that it is suddenly very audible.*]

RADIO: Good morning, fellow citizens. [*military crispness*] This is Brigadier Fadason of the armed forces calling. I bring you good tidings: the Head-of-State's hypocrisy has been detected. His government is now overthrown by the young revolutionaries —

> [NNEKA *sinks back into her seat. She bursts out in a rage.*]

NNEKA: Motherless mercenaries.

TELANI: Duty calls.

As TELANI *lugs on her cameras and stands up, lights have risen further upstage on the reception area of the Office of the Minister of Cultural Affairs.*

TELANI *steps forward.*

TELANI: I became a journalist simply because — it was the first job that came along. That's not really true, but it could've been.

Heroism was not a quality actively encouraged in my family. Father was a practical man. He had a running gag, which he never tired of repeating at parties. He would reel off a whole list of names — and he had a phenomenal memory — from all over the world, names that had one way or the other become common currency in conversations, then he would pause and ask: "What have all those names in common?" Inevitably someone was bound to respond, with some degree of impatience: "They're all folk heroes." Whereupon father would shake his head. "No," he would say, "they're all *dead* heroes."

Any idiot can be a hero, he would say, all you have to do is go up to a fellow with a gun and poke a finger in his eye. It was a warning to us kids: although he himself had been quite deeply political in his youth, he saw no gain in politics any more.

It was a lesson that stuck with me: at college, the nearest I got to being political was the time the student union magazine announced a boycott of Rothmans cigarettes because it'd been found out that its makers had been breaking the sanctions against South Africa. I gave up smoking for three days, and thereafter kept up the solidarity by doing my smoking in secret. A good thing too, because it would have been really *uncool* to have done it in public. Politics was simply not my thing.

Sooner or later we all See The Light. And when we do, we think we can change the world. That was what I thought when I first joined the *NewsDay*. Change the world. I was quickly disillusioned. We have a saying: Not even God is Wise Enough. It's the only constant in Songhai.

When the story of the schoolkids broke out,

therefore, I was more than a little interested.

I admired their courage — futile and naive as I knew it was. But I admired it. They made me feel ashamed of myself. At their age my innocence had been total, unbelievable. *They* had never been given the chance to be innocent. I'd grown up in a Songhai where the rot was settling everywhere like dust. They were born into it.

[TELANI *leaves.*]

TALATA, *the Minister's secretary, is speaking to a visitor pacing impatiently in front of her desk. The visitor is a flashily dressed* BUSINESSMAN, *briefcase at hand, well-fed-looking.*

TALATA: I'm afraid — [*reads out his name from a business card*] — Alhaji Musa Baraka, there are certain new procedures. Forms you have to fill in before you are allowed audience of His Excellency. There's also a consultation fee —
MAN: A consultation fee to see the Minister?
TALATA: A token amount really. Naturally, it varies from client to client. We determine it by income. Just as in Pay-as-you-earn.

[*The* BUSINESMAN *is growing bewildered.*]

MAN: You don't understand. I've simply come to see the Minister —
TALATA: [*matter-of-factly, without any intention of being comical*] We have a table that explains it all. Everything is rated according to income. It's called the 'face value' system. Now, at face value, how much would I say you were worth? First, we must put into consideration your pot-belly. That one is very important. It is number one. It is number one. Number two: have you a car? It is more expensive to main-

tain a pot-belly than a car. A car can at least pay for itself. A pot-belly cannot. It follows, therefore, that anybody who has a pot-belly has a car. Now, question number three, what make of car?

MAN: This is utterly —

TALATA: [*comes to the point*] Your consultation fee shall be five thousand naira —

MAN: Five thousand — for what?

[TALATA *is now busy at the typewriter.*]

TALATA: Preferably in cash, sir. Visa, Mastercard, Diners Club, American Express hesitantly accepted. Switch not even considered. No cheques, not even with a cheque card.

MAN: This is a joke. A good joke. But in poor taste.

TALATA: That will make it six thousand, sir. Cash only. No credit cards accepted. Plus five percent tax, sir. You shall, of course, be issued with a receipt.

MAN: Listen here, young lady. I have better things to do with my time than spend the day listening to . . . I telephoned this office last week. I made an appointment with you. To see the Minister.

TALATA: As you can see, sir, I'm very busy this afternoon. It's past my lunch hour and my patience can only be stretched so far.

[*Up till this moment the* BUSINESSMAN *had frankly believed it all to be a joke.*]

MAN: Are you seriously asking me to pay six thousand naira to see the Minister?

TALATA: Our rates fluctuate with the Stock Exchange, sir. If you wait another hour you may find that you have to pay less. Or even more. It all depends on the naira's performance against other currencies. The foreign exchange market figures will be out in another hour or so. You're most welcome to stay till then.

[*The* BUSINESSMAN *fills in the forms silently as she speaks. He hands them back to her.*]
Ah, you've come in connection with the Women's Day celebration.

MAN: [*pouting*] It says so on the form.

TALATA: And what might you be bidding for, sir? I ask because almost every aspect of it has been contracted out already. The invitation for tenders appeared in the papers over two weeks ago, if I remember rightly. You've come rather late in the day, you'd agree with me, especially since the event itself is barely a week away.

MAN: I tried to make an appointment over a week ago, Miss Mai Nono.

TALATA: And so you did, sir. I take it you've decided to wait for the Stock Exchange?

[*The* BUSINESSMAN *proceeds to count out wads of naira notes from his briefcase.*]

[TELANI *enters. She preoccupies herself with the pictures on the walls while the* BUSINESSMAN *is being attended to.* TALATA *issues him with a receipt.*]

[*businesslike but no longer irritable*] I'm sorry if I was a bit over the top a minute ago, Alhaji. But this consultation fee palaver only became official last week. One of the government's new economic recovery moves. Most people aren't aware of it yet. But you know how things move in this country. The government's logic is: if successive administrations have tried without success to eradicate graft, what hope had they? And then someone — His Excellency, actually — had a brainstorm: why not legalise it? Why not tax it? And that is exactly what happened. The results, even in these very early days, have been really heartwarming. His Excellency reckons that when it comes fully into effect it could easily rival petroleum as the country's leading source of income. [*conspiratorial whisper*] The word is, when the Ministry of Graft Management is created — and that's coming very soon — His Excellency might be given that portfolio.

[*She picks up the intercom.*]

Your Excellency? Your ten o'clock appointment is here. Yes, oh yes, Your Excellency, he has. And I've issued him with a receipt.

[*She drops the intercom.*]

His Excellency will be pleased to receive you in his office in a minute, Alhaji Baraka.

[*She resumes her typing.*]

You still haven't told me what aspect of the celebration you're interested in.

MAN: A subsidiary of one of my companies manufactures veils.

TELANI: [*turning sharply*] Veils? I'm sorry to barge in, but I couldn't help overhearing that.

MAN: Not at all, madam. Not at all. I was only saying a subsidiary of one of my companies is in the business of veils. Straight from Saudi Arabia, if you please. Straight from the Holy Land. You'd be surprised how many women in this country are daily embracing the veil. With the . . . very active encouragement of their husbands, of course. My wives — and I've only two, mind you — have themselves always been enthusiasts in this matter. As my dear father used to say — bless his soul — "In these days of wanton licentiousness, purdah is the last bastion of sacred womanhood." My contention —

TELANI: You have a contention, sir?

[*The* BUSINESSMAN *loses his poise momentarily.*]

MAN: Arhm, yes, yes. My contention is that in these bleak days, these days when an avenging angel

— so I've heard people say — in the form of a mysterious virus is travelling around God's world and cutting people down *en masse*, it behoves us to come together, have a total rethink of our lifestyles and —
>   [*He pauses to make sure he's got his audience enthralled. They seem to be.*]

Imagine this scenario: on the occasion of next week's celebration of National Women's Day. His Excellency climbs that podium and, having suitably cleared his throat, announces that in this country henceforth every woman, every last member of the female species, should consider herself to be in the holy state of purdah. Not for reasons parochial, oh no, not for any religious reason *please*, but for — reasons of . . . health. No doubt I shall consider it an act of good faith if the government should deem fit to call on my company to supply the first set of veils — which should be equal in number to the population of women in this country. But I assure you my interests are purely honourable.
>   [*He looks around to find* TELANI *idly flipping through the pages of a magazine. He gets the message. He packs his briefcase and heads into the Minister's office.*]

Excuse me, madam. I have business to attend to.
>   [*He leaves.*]

TALATA: [*whistling in relief*] What a pr–ick.
>   [TELANI *drops the magazine.*]

You're here for the interview with His Excellency, not so?
>   [TELANI *lights a cigarette.*]

TELANI: If I'm Telani and my car is off the road, yes. Mind you, in its time it did distinguish itself. Forty-five minutes to an emergency press conference in Ibadan and we'd still make it with plenty of time for a cigarette. And now? It's retired to a mechanic's workshop. Without so much as a by-your-leave.

TALATA: [*completely mortified*] I'm — I'm afraid I don't understand you at all.

TELANI: [*seems to snap out of it*] Oh, I'm sorry — it's my bloody car, you see. A knocked engine, last week.

TALATA: A knocked engine, you say? You're looking at about a year's salary at the least. That's if you're lucky. [*whistles*] Enough to make anyone philosophical, my sister.

[*She does a bit of typing.*]

Mind you, if you think you've got problems, wait till you hear him.

[*She cocks her head in the direction of* KIRIYO's *office.*]

On the phone to his wives and concubines.

[TELANI *is already jotting this down.*]

TELANI: He's got wives *and* concubines?

TALATA: [*eagerly*] Ten wives and concubines. It's impossible to tell which is which, seeing as he's got each one of them installed in rented apartments all over the place. Regular stipend, personal driver, gardener, houseboy, the works.

TELANI: Does he have a timetable?

TALATA: Now that's where the trouble begins. Only last week he forgot his favourite watch somewhere — couldn't remember where. I spent the entire morning phoning each of them to ask if it was at theirs by any chance.

TELANI: Did you find it?

TALATA: Not at any of the tens. Turns out there is a number eleven. A new addition to the harem. And you'd never believe it if I tell you who she is.

ACT ONE

TELANI: Should I know her?

TALATA: I rather think so. Her name is Fausa.

TELANI: Fausa!

TALATA: [*shooting frantic looks at the Minister's door*] Don't say it out so loud, please, Miss Balarabe, in the name of God. If the Minister finds out that I —

[KIRIYO *comes bursting out of his office, looking distressed. He is dragging a telephone box with him. He is followed by a puzzled-looking* BUSINESSMAN.]

KIRIYO: The lavatory, Talata, where is the lavatory?

TALATA: I beg your pardon, sir?

[KIRIYO *is obviously in shock.*]

KIRIYO: Phone call . . . ! From my senior wife . . . Coup. A change of government.

[*He thrusts the phone into* TALATA's *hands and dashes out. As* TALATA *commences to speak to the person on the line, the* BUSINESSMAN *takes his leave unceremoniously.*]

[TELANI *begins to pack her gear.*]

[*Moments later* KIRIYO *rushes back in. His flies are undone.*]

I must leave immediately, Talata, must get as far as I can from here . . . Lie low for a while until things become clearer . . . Until the haze clears and one knows who the new boys are . . .

[TELANI *is on the point of leaving.*]

TELANI: A coup, Mr Minister?

TALATA: No need for any of that, Your Excellency, you didn't give Madam the chance to finish what she was saying.

[TELANI *is by the door.*]

She was only saying that she'd heard it on the radio that there was a coup attempt which was instantly crushed this morning —

TELANI: [*returning*] Even I could've told you that.

KIRIYO: [*hyperventilating*] Of course, of course, I did hear her mention that it'd been successfully repelled. I was only demonstrating to my brilliant new friend, Alhaji, here . . . a coup situation drill . . . Are you with me, Alhaji?

    [*He has only now realised that the* BUSINESSMAN *has fled.*]

Poor fellow took fright, I suppose. Can't say I blame him. Most naughty of me.

    [TALATA *is frantically trying to catch* KIRIYO'*s attention.*]

TALATA: Excuse me, sir —

KIRIYO: Something in your eye, Talata?

TALATA: Your garage is open, sir.

    [*She makes surreptitious signs in the direction of* KIRIYO'*s crotch.*]

KIRIYO: My what? Are you sure you're — ?

    [*He accidentally looks downward and it suddenly dawns on him what she has been attempting to tell him. He takes it in his stride.*]

Oh yes, Talata, indeed . . . My garage — did you notice the rather elegant new model Mercedes Benz parked there? A surprise, actually. A wedding gift for my dear new wife.

    [*He zips up with immense dignity.*]

Straight from Germany.

    [TELANI *is furiously scribbling away.*]

TELANI: Ah, getting married, Your Excellency. Who's the lucky woman?

    [KIRIYO *notices her for the first time.*]

KIRIYO: Who are you? Who is this?

    [*He makes a grab for* TELANI'*s notebook.*]

A journalist. I should've guessed. I hope you're a good journalist. I loathe bad journalists, those ones who only think of ways of making trouble, making life uncomfortable for hard-working, God-fearing people like myself. All you people

ACT ONE

know how to do is criticize, criticize, criticize. Parasites, the lot of you. Feeding on the misery of others. Personally, I think it's an unpardonable waste of money employing people to be journalists. Talk of *paying* a graffiti terrorist to deface public walls. *Paying!*

[*All through this outburst he has been leafing perfunctorily through* TELANI's *notebook. He freezes, then smiles.*]

Congratulations, you've found me out, Miss — Balarabe. A security leak, no doubt. But I'll deal with that in good time. Shall we step into the confessional? You have found Halilu Tijanni.

[*He carefully rips out the pages from the notebook.*]

These are of no use to you, I'm sure you'd realise that. Your editor is too sensible a person to allow such a blatantly criminal invasion of one's private life to be carried in her paper.

TELANI: Quite frankly, I don't understand this —

KIRIYO: You may not be aware of this but under the new Public Service Laws all senior civil servants seeking to have more than a certain number of wives are required to seek presidential sanction . . . Clarification of their individual quota —

TELANI: There's a quota system, then?

[*Her sarcasm is not lost on him.*]

KIRIYO: Quota system, presidential go-ahead . . . Call it what you will. I had to wait for that before going public.

TELANI: Fausa is —

KIRIYO: Sixteen, yes. It might surprise you to know that I'm actually aware of that. She's like a daughter to me, you know. I've known her since —

TELANI: Are you in the habit of going to bed with your daughter, then?

KIRIYO: Yes —

[*He has said it before realising what the question had been. He swallows hard. His fury is rabid.*]

Lady, I'll have you know that I'm not one of your run-of-the-mill easily intimidated government officials —

TELANI: [*very angry now*] And all those kids locked up because of her?

KIRIYO: Not because of her, Miss Balarabe. Certainly not because of her. That lot are no better than a gang of common criminals. They need some sense knocked into their tiny little skulls, that's what they need.

[*As KIRIYO finishes his speech they all go into freeze.*]

Lights rise on a flashback.

EBENEZER, TIMO, MODUPE *and* NEHUSTA *are on the doorstep of the Ibrahimas' house.*

TIMO: Do you reckon Fausa might be in there right this very moment and her father was only having us on when he said she wasn't?

[EBENEZER *is pacing restlessly around.*]

NEHUSTA: I really don't know what to believe. Plus, it doesn't matter whether she's in there or not, our demand is simple and straightforward: give us Fausa. He says she's with Halilu. We've been to Halilu's place — he's moved. So what to do? We wait patiently here until Fausa's produced.

[EBENEZER *is furiously kicking a rubber ball around.*]

TIMO: He's rather taking his time calling the police.

NEHUSTA: I told you he only wanted to get past us, that's why he started threatening us with the police.

EBENEZER: If you lot had listened to me we'd have seized

the old fool when he came out. I mean, I'm all for this non-violent protest thing, believe me, but look where it's got us so far. Fucking nowhere, that's where. And how long have we been at it? Over a week now. Carrying poxy placards all over the place. And what have we achieved? Fuck all. Sweet F.A., that's what. We've only succeeded in being ignored by everybody. So we've been in the press; the school's been shut . . . But how much closer are we to tracking down Fausa — let alone freeing her — than we were on the first day? Not an inch closer, so help me God. Not one bloody inch closer. No-one cares, no-one gives a *bazooka joe*. As far as they're concerned, we're just a bunch of juvenile delinquents bored with school work, which I was, to be honest, and I'm beginning to suspect that the only reason many people joined the protest when we first started was because they wanted what happened this morning — closure of the school, another holiday. And now that school's been closed . . . [*waves to indicate*] . . . that's what they were after: a bloody holiday. This morning after assembly they were bending over backwards to assure us they'd be here tonight. But where are they all? I'll tell you where they are: as far from here as they could possibly be. [*Pause.*] I still think we should've seized the old idiot, if you ask me.

MODUPE: And do what with him?

EBENEZER: You've heard of the term exchange-of-hostages?

NEHUSTA: All you'll end up exchanging is your school khaki for a prison term. Mark my word.

[*A* POLICE OFFICER *enters.*]

OFFICER: Well, well, alleluia. I thought there were more of them, Mr Ibrahima. [*takes a backward glance offstage*] Oh well, never mind, never mind. Alleluia. [*turns to the* STUDENTS] I think Mr Ibrahima is a bit shy of you guys, he's very upset at the sudden interest you've taken in his doorstep. He was in quite a state when he arrived at the station an hour ago. Absolutely flustered. Kept mumbling about this gang of hooligans who'd invaded his home and were laying siege for him. Alleluia, I said, alleluia. We couldn't make sense of anything he said. Not until he mentioned his name. Ibrahima. And we said, ah, the Fausa girl's father. Alleluia. And we said to him, these invaders, they wouldn't happen to be the same people who'd been going around all week accusing him of abducting his own daughter, would they? And he said, as a matter of fact, they were none other. Alleluia, alleluia. So we decided to escort him back home so that we could personally invite you to the station for a chat . . . This whole area is surrounded by my colleagues, of course, so I wouldn't advise anyone to entertain any thoughts of dashing off. I hope I make myself clear. Alleluia.

EBENEZER: Officer, why do you keep saying that?

OFFICER: Alleluia? Let me put it this way: a few months ago what I'd have said when I saw you lot would've been something like: "Are you the *four-letter-word* bastards who've been making a nuisance of themselves on the streets instead of staying in their classrooms?"

EBENEZER: You mean you'd swear at us as in: "Are you the fucking bastards . . . ?"

OFFICER: Alleluia. Not only that, I'd have beaten you to a pulp by now. But I've recently received the Lord into my life. I've seen the light. Whenever the swearing itch comes upon me I say alleluia instead.

ACT ONE

EBENEZER: [*to the others*] You should've fucking listened to me.

OFFICER: Excuse me, sir, are you the one called Ebenezer — the spokesman?

> [*He gets a 'so what?' expression from EBENEZER. The POLICE OFFICER brings out a pocket-sized bible.*]

"Vengeance is mine; I shall repay, saith the Lord."

> [*He clasps shut the bible.*]

Not only have you committed a crime and induced others into crime, you have sinned and led others astray.

> [*He kicks EBENEZER in the groin.*]

God loves a penitent sinner.

> [*He kicks him again.*]

But first we must make you penitent.

Lights spring on TELANI *and she comes out of her freeze as the flashback ends.*
TELANI fixes KIRIYO with a long stare.

TELANI: I'd like to commit a vileness on you and your type.

KIRIYO: [*full of sarcasm*] Shoot me?

TELANI: No. Not me, you won't be getting any favours from me. Bastards like you are the strongest argument against capital punishment.

KIRIYO: Get out of my office.

TELANI: I am, Mr Minister, but don't you for a single moment think I shan't be coming back.

KIRIYO: [*beside himself*] Get out of this building. Now. This very moment.

> [*Instant blackout.*]

END OF ACT ONE

ACT TWO

The editorial suite of the NewsDay-on-Sunday.
NNEKA, TELANI *and* ZAK *are in conference.*

NNEKA: I'm prepared to give you the benefit of the doubt, Miss Balarabe. Unfortunately, this query is from the readers, not from the editor's office.

TELANI: When your secretary brought the letters to my attention yesterday I was quite struck by the uncanny similarity of the diction throughout. And they're all typed . . . from the same typewriter.

NNEKA: [*to* ZAK] Is she trying to suggest something?

ZAK: I hope you're not trying to suggest anything, Miss Balarabe.

TELANI: I'm merely saying that the whole matter reeks of a personal vendetta.

NNEKA: I have nothing against you, Miss Balarabe. You are hard-working — when you want to be — you are a good reporter, an even better photographer. There's just one tiny problem. [*Pause.*] You're becoming too well-known for your own good. You're letting it get to your head. Worst of all, you think you're a star —

TELANI: Mrs Alakija-Brown —

NNEKA: You suffer from delusions of grandeur. Believe me, I know about these things. Happens even to the best of us. You're afflicted with a condition commonly known as the star complex. Nothing that a generous dose of good old humility wouldn't cure, mind. You think you're a star. What you don't seem to realise is that stars are up there . . . and you are down here.

ZAK: Hear, hear.

NNEKA: Having given the matter a great deal of thought, having carefully considered these letters before me, and bearing in mind that the customer is always right, and having accepted that in the present instance Customer is synonymous with Reader — and vice versa — I have, with utmost hesitation, decided that the column *Telani on Sunday* no longer reflects the exalted values of the *NewsDay* and has thus rendered itself irrelevant.

TELANI: Wait a minute —

NNEKA: No, *you* wait a minute: [*as if reading out a memo*] Starting from next Sunday, therefore, *Telani on Sunday* shall cease to exist. Miss Balarabe shall return to her former post of news correspondent subject to further action.

TELANI: There's been a misunderstanding, Miss — Mrs Alakija-Brown.

NNEKA: I'm afraid, Miss Balarabe, the matter is closed.

TELANI: Mrs Alakija-Brown.

NNEKA: Closed, Miss Balarabe. [*A thoughtful pause.*] I really don't understand you at all, you know. I thought — used to think — I did. I thought: there's a young woman full of ambition, a woman who knows what she wants. But I was wrong. Let me tell you one thing: all this hoity-toity idealism is only so much hot air.

TELANI: [*quietly, guardedly optimistic*] What about this story of the Minister's new bride?

NNEKA: [*with an air of total exasperation*] It's ours to look but not to see, Miss Balarabe. Ours to do but not to question. We're not in the business of poking noses into closets. Does that sound familiar?

TELANI: Yes it does.

ZAK: It's a matter of great sensitivity, yes. Has to be handled carefully, yes.

ACT TWO

NNEKA: That's the spirit, my dear Features. That's the spirit. Tact and diplomacy. [*to* TELANI] Perhaps there's a lesson to be learnt there?

TELANI: Just this story, Mrs Editor! Just this one!

ZAK: You don't seem to understand, Miss Balarabe. Certain things are better left unsaid.

[TELANI *swings on him.*]

TELANI: Keep your squeak out of this!

[ZAK *springs up in an awkward boxing posture.*]

NNEKA: Mr Features! Miss Balarabe, one more thing you must learn to understand is that we do not all have wealthy fathers to fall back on.

TELANI: Keep my father out of this —

NNEKA: If we had done that in the first place you wouldn't be here now and being — holy. You probably wouldn't have even made the short list.

TELANI: I have to say this, Mrs Alakija-Brown, that was pure drivel. [*Pause.*] One more thing — are we doing anything *at all* about the Ajegunle kids?

NNEKA: Do anything?

TELANI: Instance: the police have categorically refused to release them on bail.

NNEKA: Point of correction: the situation is that none of the families involved has so far shown any inclination towards producing the bail money.

TELANI: Point of correction: the Lagos Branch of the Market Women's Union did produce the amount requested. I know this because I went to the police station on their behalf.

Lights rise on the Police Station.
A group of POLICEMEN *are playing a game of draughts. In the background — and intermittently throughout this scene — the voices of the* SCHOOL-

> CHILDREN *can be heard raised in song.*
>
> POLICEMAN 1 *is attending to a man who has come to report an incident. It is the* BUSINESSMAN *whom we last met in the Minister's office.*

POLICE 1: So Oga me, Alhaji, what time you say you reach home come discover di incident?

> [*His whole attention is on his colleagues' game.*]

Ah, Leo, see me see trouble o, Leo. Wetin you thin' say you de play so? See me see trouble o.

> [*He turns with decided impatience to the* BUSINESSMAN.]

I ask you kweshun. You get lockjaw for mouth? I say which time you reach home?

MAN: Around four this morning.

POLICE 1: A.m. or p.m.? Leo. Lee-yooo, why you come play that hand now, you no see say na open you open yansh for am so? You fool o, you dis man, you fool too much. Oga, you hear me so? I say a.m. or p.m.?

MAN: I said four this morning, Officer. If only you'd give me a fraction of your attention —

> [POLICEMAN 1 *whistles incredulously at a tactical error he's noticed in* POLICEMAN 2's *move.*]

POLICE 1: Na lie, I no believe my eye, which kind nonsense game you de play so? Abi na hungry don turn you so? Look, make you comot make I show Sergeant how to play game.

> [*He pushes* POLICEMAN 2 *aside and takes his place. He turns to the harried* BUSINESSMAN *and gestures to* POLICEMAN 2.]

Tell Corporal Leo wetin you jus' tell me.

MAN: Officer!

> [POLICEMAN 2 *is now manning the incidents desk.*]

POLICE 2: Don't mind the Corporal, ya Alhaji, he always

gets that way this time of month. Simply means he's broke, he means no harm. He's a nice man when you get to know him.

MAN: My Ikoyi house was burgled last night, Officer. Swept stark clean, and I mean, they actually had the guts, after carting away all my property, to hoover the house from top to bottom.

[*The* SCHOOLCHILDREN's *voices have now risen to an unbearable pitch.*]

POLICE 2: Just a moment, sir.

[*He leans in the direction of the cells offstage.*]

Shut up, you tiny swine!

[TELANI *enters, dragging a bulging sack. She practically collides with* POLICEMAN 2, *who is gently leading the* BUSINESSMAN, *who now looks positively shell-shocked, towards the door.*]

I'd count myself lucky if I were you, sir. Slow Poison Joe is the last of a rare breed of gentlemen-burglars left in this city. He's a decent man too, a man of his word. You're most fortunate he decided to leave this note for you. That means he means for you to get your property back. Subject, of course, to a suitable arrangement between the two of you. I'd suggest that you dip right down into your pocket. No change is too small. Slow Poison Joe take that one resemble God. He loves a generous giver.

MAN: Oh my God, oh my God.

POLICE 2: Believe me, sir, I do understand your predicament, how anxious you are to be reconciled with your beloved property. But you'll have to exercise patience until next Saturday. That's when he's due here next — for a game of — [*nods in the direction of the draughts board*] Don't you worry at all. I go de here, you can rely on me to put in a good word on your behalf.

> [*He pushes the* BUSINESSMAN *out and turns to face* TELANI.]

Good morning, madam, can we be of any assistance to you?

TELANI: I've come to stand bail for the schoolchildren you're holding here.

POLICE 2: [*appraising her*] Who you be? [*leans towards the cells*] Shut up, you little shits, you hear!

> [TELANI *hands him a press card.*]

TELANI: A family friend — to one of them — [*thinks*] — Ebenezer Manchok.

POLICE 2: Why are they not here themselves?

TELANI: Here themselves — sorry, who?

POLICE 2: His parents? What are you doing here if his own kin and blood couldn't be bothered?

> [TELANI *picks up the sack and empties it on the floor. Wads of banknotes pour out.*]

TELANI: Because they haven't got a bank manager who'd grant them such facilities. I understand that you no longer accept cheques here either?

> [POLICEMAN 2 *stares open-mouthed at the heap of money.*]

POLICE 1: **Alhamdullilahi!**

> [*As* POLICEMAN 2 *goes on his knees to count the money all the* POLICEMEN *abandon their game to join him.*]

POLICE 3: **Ten thousan'!**

> [*He does a dance routine around the heap and sings.*]

T'obirin ba dara, Bio lewa

ALL: *simultaneously*] **Mo lefi ten thousan' fe!***

**Variation on a popular 1950s Highlife song: So long as she's got manners / I don't care how my woman looks / I'll pay the dowry / Even if it's ten thousand!*

ACT TWO

TELANI: Well?
POLICE 3: Well what?
TELANI: Bring out the kids.
POLICE 2: Exactly which kids do you have in mind, madam?
TELANI: I don't mean to be disrespectful, Officer, but apart from yourselves, how many kids are there in this station?
POLICE 2: I sorry, madam, but if you mean those lack-of-no-home-training children in there, I'm afraid we can't let you have them.
TELANI: Why not?
POLICE 3: Orders from up yonder. Come las' night. No bail under any circumstantial.
TELANI: Shee-it. This — this has to be a joke.
POLICE 2: Look, madam, we can fit to let you see them if you want. But as for bailing them — even God Almighty cannot fit to do it at this point in time.

[*He turns to* POLICEMAN 1.]

Bring one of those children make madam see how well we de treat them.

[*He turns to* TELANI.]

Which one did you say you knew? Oh yes, Manchok.

[POLICEMAN 1 *gives him an 'Are you sure?' expression and goes out.*]

Don't believe any of those bad stories you hear about us. I tell you. Na fabricate, all of them. Police na flesh and blood like yourself.

[POLICEMAN 1 *returns. He is pushing in front of him an apparition. It is a human being, of course. The entire head area is covered in bandages. It seems almost like a turban, except for the caked blood. Where the mouth should have been there's a generous distension of flesh.*]

TELANI: [*horrified*] Ebenezer?
> [*The apparition nods.*]
POLICE 1: [*in response to nasty looks from* POLICEMAN 2 *and* POLICEMAN 3] Not you say make I bring am come?
POLICE 2: I'm sorry, madam, I didn't realise he was the one you meant. Honest to God, madam — on my father's grave — no, he's still alive —
TELANI: What have you beasts done to him?
> [POLICEMAN 1 *leads* EBENEZER *back to the cells.*]
POLICE 3: Honest to God, we didn't lay a finger on him — I admit he was roughed up a bit during the arrest — but that was nothing really — simply standard procedure. He only lost one tooth — what's that to a seventeen-year-old kid? Now, what you saw — that was caused by one of our older clients — veterans, if you like. The broken head — that's a speciality of Super Kali Ali Baba — he used to be a butcher, you see, until the day he tried his skills on an irate customer. The customer escaped, but without his left ear.

The editorial suite of the NewsDay-on-Sunday.

NNEKA: Good point, Miss Balarabe. Good point. The police — who, second to the army, practically own this country — had the wisdom to develop cold feet when they sensed the magnitude of the might involved . . . And you — you expect us ordinary civilian mortals to do what?
ZAK: Bell the cat.
TELANI: They're mere juveniles, these kids, and there's no justification for keeping them in custody, they're no criminals —
NNEKA: They soon will be.

ACT TWO

TELANI: I take it then that there's to be no story on them in the *NewsDay*?

NNEKA: That would be a wrong and rather hasty conclusion. There'll be a story. What's more, it's already written: an editorial —

[NNEKA *passes a proof sheet to* TELANI.]

TELANI: [*with growing incredulity*] This is a joke, no? [*reads*] This is a joke? [*reads*] "Rascals . . . juvenile delinquents . . . reactionary dissidents . . . extremists . . . rotten-eggs-that-must-be-weeded-out . . . master-criminals-in-the-making . . ."

ZAK: Brilliantly written, if I may say so. Amazingly bold. Go for the jugular, that's what I say.

TELANI: You'll be endangering the lives of these children if you publish this. I hope you remember that whenever you've finished yes-sirring.

NNEKA: Prudent choice of words. I take it Daddy's already found *us* another job?

TELANI: These are mere kids, for God's sake. You shouldn't use them as props in your career. They are this country's future . . .

NNEKA: So are mosquitoes.

ZAK: So is malaria fever.

[NNEKA *hands* TELANI *a standard resignation letter.*]

NNEKA: If you'll sign above the line there, please.

TELANI: You'll have to fire me, I'm afraid.

[*She tears up the letter and begins to leave.*]

NNEKA: Very well, you're fired, Telani Balarabe.

[NNEKA *and* ZAK *watch her leave.*]

What on earth is the matter with that girl?

ZAK: [*absently*] They sometimes get that way just before menopause, sudden flights of depression.

NNEKA: Who?

ZAK: Women, of course. I read it somewhere.

[NNEKA *glares suspiciously at him.*]
NNEKA: Did you? How very interesting. [*with a touch of irritable impatience*] She's only thirty, you idiot.
ZAK: Yes, the pity of it. Twenty years of depression? I'd see a doctor if I were in her shoes.

An elderly WOMAN, *in* iro *and* buba, *is shown bathed in a spotlight.*
TELANI *steps forward.*

TELANI: In time to come those schoolchildren were to prove to be Songhai's future. The last dregs of oil — the country's main source of income — had been dredged out of the bowels of the earth. If you stood on a hill and shouted aloud for help only your voice would come bouncing back, mocking, in a thousand echoes of your desperation. So with the national treasury. It was so empty you could hear a coin drop. After decades of a feverish and relentless assault, the national cake had turned to dust.

Songhai lay in desolation. It was as in the aftermath of war. There were howlings of rage, of pure, helpless anger all over the land.

And from this rubble arose a group of men and women: full of life and brimming with ideas; articulate and zestful; astute and with an unshaking integrity; inspired, and endowed with the gift to lead. Many of them had been — the Ajegunle children. The kids who had marched — seemingly in vain at the time — for a girl called Fausa. Their names were not necessarily Nehusta, Ebenezer, Modupe or even Timo. Or maybe they were.

Through the strength of their vision and the grittiness of their conviction they pulled Song-

ACT TWO

hai up from the ruins of defeat and slowly but surely began to lead her back to the path of hope.
[*She leaves.*]

The WOMAN *in iro and* buba *begins her speech. Lights should only gradually rise around her to reveal a delegation of Women's Union leaders, who are listening to the* WOMAN *in rapt attention. It should only be revealed towards the end of the* WOMAN's *speeech that* TELANI *is in the group.*

WOMAN: Your Excellency, was it not our people who said that when you see a person in a hurry, you should know that they carry a burden on their back? We are all gathered here in your office this morning — women all of us, mothers, sisters, daughters, wives, grandmothers — from all over this big country of ours. My calendar tells me that today is a Friday, a weekday. Last week around this time I was in my shop in Sabo taking care of business. I was no less busy the week before that. The same can be said for most of my sisters here. Why then have we all chosen to abandon our livelihood this particular Friday morning and head for your office?
[*We now see* KIRIYO, *a study in attentiveness, listening, with* TALATA *beside him.*]
Is it because we have nothing to do? Is it because we have no jobs? No, Your Excellency. The reason we've all come here this morning in such a hurry is because we have a burden on our backs.

We are mothers, many of us here, we have children: trees we've planted with our blood, plants we've nurtured with our sweat. We know also that His Excellency has children himself, is a father many times. That is why we find it hard to understand all this. That is why we've come to ask: why has he locked up our children and thrown away the keys? Was it not only proper that they should show concern over the fate of a mate of theirs? What crime have they committed that is so bad they must now share the same bed with murderers and robbers? And, finally, is it true what we hear, that our daughter Fausa is indeed His Excellency's new bride, or is the story the work of slanderers and bad-mouthers who, Peace Be Upon The Prophet's Name, will surely be struck down by lightning?

> [As the WOMAN finishes to general applause KIRIYO steps forward. He will also be under a spotlight when he makes his speech so that, although the pretence is that he is addressing the delegation, he will in fact be facing the audience.]

KIRIYO: Madam Chairlady, National Union of Market Women, Ladies. It gladdens my heart immensely to see so many of you here today. In fact —

> [TALATA leans into the spotlight and whispers into his ear.]

I have just been informed that the traffic jam which delayed my arrival at the office this morning may have been caused by the influx into the city of women from all over our great land attending this —

> [He lapses into mumbling. Another whisper from TALATA. KIRIYO blanches but quickly regains composure.]

I have just been informed that there are an estimated hundred thousand women outside this office at this moment.

ACT TWO

[Clearly he is bewildered.]
I must say that I find this very, very encouraging indeed. More so, since in a few days' time we shall all be gathered at a venue not too far from here to celebrate the Sixth National Women's Day — our preparations for which I shall like to briefly dwell upon with your kind permission. It was a task — be it noted — the prospect of which filled me with not a little trepidation. Do not misunderstand me, please: I have nothing against women. In fact I love women — some of my best wives — are women.

[Whisper from TALATA.]
All of my best wives are women.

[Another whisper.]
All of my wives are women . . . I mean to say, some of my best friends are women. My mother was a woman . . . Yet I was filled with a certain unease when I was asked to take charge of the organisation of this august occasion. For, you see, women are hard to please.

[A tentative hum from the WOMEN.]
Bearing that in mind, therefore, I trod with caution. I was in consultation with some of the best minds on women's affairs in the land . . . And our grand celebration next week — the like of which has never been witnessed before, not to my knowledge anyhow — will be the well-earned result of all those sleepless nights. My secretary will testify to this. No, no, not the sleepless nights. Well, she did spend a few sleepless nights too. But not with me. Please, please . . . let me finish. Our theme for this year is 'Obedience'. You'll notice that I haven't said 'Obadiah'. I said 'Obedience'.

[He pauses — for applause — then goes on when he realises it is not forthcoming.]

I didn't think it was that funny either. But my speechwriters insisted . . . Obedience . . . at home, at work and at play. We did not stumble upon this, ladies, I assure you. It wasn't an off-hand decision. We sat down for a long time and deliberated. Our nation is today suffering from the plague of indiscipline, there is a rash, an epidemic of gross indiscipline that has infected every aspect of our lives. From the dregs of this society to our best minds. What is needed is discipline . . . And this, ladies, is what we lack. Let me assure you all, here and now: things cannot go on this way. And I address this to you women: you must change . . .

[*He is getting carried away.*]

In all my time — in all my two score years and ten — I've never seen such a breakdown in the order of things. When I was a schoolboy I behaved like a schoolboy. But I did not throw down my books to go roaming the streets carrying placards and singing inane songs because the parents of one of my schoolmates had decided that it was time someone made an honest woman of her. I went to school conscientiously, read my books, obeyed my teachers, passed my examinations. And I did not listen to Bob Marley music.

> [*He swings round on his heels, gives a curt bow, and begins to leave, followed by the delegation who do not yet realise that he has come to the end of his speech. This scene would be enhanced by the use of choreography. The effect for which to strive would be a James Brown stage routine, with its spontaneity and near banal melodrama but also with its well-finished orchestration.*]
>
> [*The* WOMAN *runs after* KIRIYO.]

ACT TWO

WOMAN: Mr Minister, Mr Minister —
KIRIYO: I forgive but I never forget —
WOMAN: Mr Minister, sir —
KIRIYO: To spare the rod is to conserve the forests —
WOMAN: But you can't treat us this way, Minister Kiriyo —
KIRIYO: Keep the land green, use recycled paper —
WOMAN: Eyi koma da o, Mista minista* —
KIRIYO: Send toxic waste right back to Downing Street —
WOMAN: Minister Kiriyo!
  [KIRIYO *swings round and faces her.*]
KIRIYO: All well and good, my dear mothers. But can we afford to spare the rod and spoil the child?
WOMAN: You speak in proverbs, Minister Kiriyo.
KIRIYO: No, my dear mothers, we cannot afford to spare the rod and spoil the child. That would be kobo wise but naira foolish. Because that very child will grow up spoilt, undiscerning, a cultural guerrilla, bereft of any redeeming values. He will grow up without any principles, let alone ecological principles. In other words, my dear mothers, that very child whom we spared the rod will grow up and cut down all the trees of sapele, sell them as firewood. And smoke marijuana with the money. Is that the kind of society we want to build? Is that the sort of legacy we'd like to bequeath to future generations?
  [*He pulls out a sheet and reads.*]
"You are invited this Sunday to the national stadium when these so-called Ajegunle children shall each be administered with fifty strokes apiece of the best. For those of you who are unable to come to the stadium I'm pleased to announce that you'll have the opportunity of watching the proceedings live on your screens at

---

* This is not proper, Mr Minister!

home. There'll be a photo session with the felons afterwards, so do come with your cameras and camcorders. Good day."

[TELANI *steps forward and pulls him back.*]

TELANI: Not for you, Kiriyo.

[*As the* WOMEN *descend on* KIRIYO: *Instant black. All freeze.*]

The radio comes on. A voice cuts through a music programme.

RADIO: We are interrupting this programme to bring you an important news item. Songi has gone up in flames. A crowd of women, over a hundred thousand strong and reportedly led by former newspaper columnist and photographer, Telani Balarabe, literally torched the city this morning when they abducted the Federal Minister of Cultural Affairs, His Excellency Dr Olatide Kiriyo from his Ikeja offices. It is believed that the women had originally come with the intention of pleading with the Minister for the release of the Ajegunle children. The Minister was stripped of his clothing and taken to the studios of the National Television Authority where in front of live television cameras he was whipped within an inch of his life. The protest, which was initially devoid of aggression towards public property, was later hijacked by vandals and looters, most of them male. A presidential spokeswoman said that the rioting was nothing short of a criminal insurrection and that it would be treated as such.

[*Then we hear gunshots offstage. And screams. These will go on for nearly a minute, until the radio comes on once more.*

ACT TWO

The sound of applause comes from the radio.]
[*In the near total darkness we can make out TELANI's figure, hunched over in a chair as at the beginning of the play, a cigarette smouldering between her fingers.*]

RADIO: And now to the next item on our programme on this occasion of the Sixth National Women's Day: a beauty pageant, I've been made to understand, an exhibition of the True African Woman which is presented to you courtesy of the Army Officers' Wives' Association. In the course of the pageant we shall be treated to demonstrations on such very important family issues as: 'How to greet your husband' [a] in the morning [b] in the evening [c] in the morning or evening and [d] in the morning and evening. Other issues to be tackled — no less important, please — include 'How to speak to a man', 'How to dress properly on a date', 'How to win a man's heart', 'How to know when he's serious', 'How to know when he's not', 'How to behave on the bridal night', 'How to find out when he's cheating' and 'How to win him back' . . . The exhibition shall then be rounded up with a word of advice to aspiring young ladies from the controversial Lady 'E' herself. Our dear First Lady — who is a self-avowed feminist and at the vanguard of that most worthy of causes — will once again rock the establishment with a lecture entitled 'The fastest way to a man's heart is through his stomach'. The indomitable Lady 'E' — as she's fondly known to us all — has a reputation for pulling no punches when making a view. Not even members of her family have escaped her searching eye. Only last month she caused quite a storm when she was heard to refer in public to one of her sons as a 'spoilt brat' when he failed to offer his seat to a stewardess on a fully booked Songhaian Airways domestic flight. The berated young man put his unbecoming behaviour down to the fact that it was a domestic flight and the 'No Smoking' sign was on. A big round of applause for Lady 'E' . . . Your presence here today is an honour, Madame.

[*Pause after the applause.*]

A minor technical hitch here, I'm afraid, chiefs, ladies and gentlemen. The pageant shall not be taking place as yet. I've just been informed that it was re-scheduled after the programmes had gone to press. Our sincere apologies to Lady 'E'. The pageant, and Lady 'E's talk, will now take place after the Minister's opening speech. This means, of course, that the Pemperempe Dance Troupe, which was earlier scheduled to perform last . . . [*Pause.*] . . . will now be performing last. You'll be pleased to know that Her Excellency and her aides have finally managed to escape the impossible traffic jam on Third Mainland Bridge which had earlier prevented them from making it here . . . Here she comes, chiefs, ladies and gentlemen, put your hands together for our new Minister of Cultural Affairs, who until two days ago was editor of the *NewsDay-on-Sunday* . . . Gentlemen, ladies, chiefs, here comes Chief Mrs Nneka Alakija-Brown . . .

Towards the end of the above speech SSS 1 *and* SSS 2 *enter. Lights come on as* SSS 1 *reaches for the knob of the radio and turns it off. He is dressed as he was when we first met him, except that he has lost his clean-cut, smooth-talking demeanour. His shirt appears to be smudged with bloodstains. He and his subordinate are looking almost as glazed as* TELANI.

TELANI *gazes at the bloodstains with a questioning but disinterested look.*

SSS 1: [*answering her unspoken question*] My mother asked me to cut a fowl at Christmas once. My first time, I trapped its wings firmly under my foot and tied its claws with a string. I took the knife to it and felt its flesh and its veins and the pipes in its neck burst at the touch of steel. With one panicky stroke I separated the head from the body. The blood gushed out freely and I felt a sense of elevation. I'd singlehandedly — I was ten at the time — killed a chicken. Or so I thought — that it was dead. The moment I let go of its wings it practically came back to life. There I was, clutching at a kitchen knife, mouth agape, as this fowl flew frantically around the compound, sprinkling blood everywhere as it searched for its head.
[*He picks a piece of grime off his shirt.*]
Cell number eight, Miss Balarabe. An ox of a fellow. He reminded me again of that headless fowl from so many years ago. [*turns to* SSS 2] How many rounds did it take to finish him off?

SSS 2: A whole cartridge, sir, that man get strong juju.

SSS 1: A whole cartridge, Telani. I've been in this business long enough to lose my sense of being surprised, and I can tell you that I've seldom seen anyone rise up again after that initial slug in the pith of the brain. This man, not only did it take an entire cartridge to make him still — and I'm talking here of brains splattered all over the wall, like an abattoir, but you don't want to hear that do you? — the fellow was still twitching when the meat van came. Such a man, such a strong man. If I could be strong to a tenth — no, a hundredth — degree of that man when my time comes, I'll be the happiest man in hell. [*pulls up a chair and sits*] I have news for you. His Excellency does not want you executed.

TELANI: [*genuinely surprised*] Why is that?

SSS 1: He was on the phone to me a while ago. Something to do with a brilliant photograph of him you took some months ago. He said to me — and I'll quote his exact words — "People like her are more use to the nation alive than dead." He wants you to know that in principle he has nothing against setting you free. In fact . . .

[*He bends down and unlocks the chain around her legs.*]

You're free to walk out of this room this very minute. This very minute. There's a boat out there waiting — by presidential fiat. Just under half an hour you would be in Songi free as a bird. But . . . [*produces the list once more*] . . . we ask one tiny favour of you: that you append your signature to this piece of paper. I know, I know, we've been through this before. But I'm being very frank with you now.

[*He assumes a voice that suggests a sharing of confidence.*]

This list in my hand is a carefully compiled list of some of the most dangerous enemies of our fatherland. As I'm sure you know — even if you insist you don't recognise any of the names — most of them are highly visible figures, public figures if you wish. They're not the sort of people who disappear and no-one says a word. They must be apprehended publicly, lawfully,

ACT TWO

and in a manner that will not arouse suspicion. That is why we need you to sign this statement.

TELANI: And incriminate them. Why me?

SSS 2: They are already incriminated. What we want from you is corroboration. Why you? Simple: you're a nationally respected journalist. Who better?

   [TELANI *takes the paper from him and stretches out her hand for a pen. He hurriedly digs one out from his pocket, showing surprise.*]

TELANI: Tell me, Mr Ari, what happened to the schoolkids?

SSS 1: [*smiles, pleased*] You've said my name for the first time. Call me Samsa, please. None of that 'Mr' business. Which schoolchildren do you mean?

TELANI: You know which ones I mean, Mr Ari.

SSS 1: The truth is ... [*Pause. He is struck by an idea.*] ... this is a big organisation, Miss Balarabe. My territory does not extend beyond this island. And here we do not have facilities for children. The sort of traffic that frequents this route does not often go back. Perhaps when you've regained your liberty you'll be in a position to commence an investigation into their whereabouts?

TELANI: Are you telling me that they are missing?

SSS 1: I haven't said any such thing. I —

TELANI: Are you saying they might be dead?

SSS 1: Miss Balarabe, you are getting hysterical.

TELANI: You've killed them, haven't you? [*lashes out at him*] You murderers, murderers, murderers.

   [SSS 1 *disentangles himself after a heated struggle. He heads for the door in a rage. He pauses at the door.*]

SSS 1: You have forty-five minutes to make up your

mind, Miss Balarabe, your lease is about to expire.

TELANI: Ninety, you mean. I've heard about your forty-five minute interval 'timetable'. Or are your men so thirsty for my blood that they will skip Cell nine and come for me in his stead?

SSS 1: Cell nine is empty at this moment.

TELANI: I didn't hear him being taken away. I didn't hear any noise.

SSS 1: He was a Rufus.

TELANI: Rufus?

SSS 1: A Rufus. His neck snapped at dawn.

TELANI: [*quietly*] You hung him.

SSS 1: No. He hung himself.

TELANI: Oh.

SSS 1: Forty-five minutes.

[*He leaves.*]

[*As the lights go into gradual fade,* TELANI *flicks on the radio. We hear the first few words of a coup announcement.*]

[*Dark.*]

THE END

Also available from Amber Lane Press

Heidi Thomas   INDIGO

Possession and betrayal are the principal themes of this vividly poetic drama. Set in the late 18th century, *Indigo* is the story of two young men: Ide, an African prince, and William, son of a Liverpudlian slave merchant. Both are caught up in the ruthless commerce of the slave trade. Ideals are destroyed and innocence confounded before the play is brought to its brutal conclusion.

Caryl Phillips   THE SHELTER

"The postcard had immediately seized my eye: a white woman's face, probably that of a woman of thirty or thirty-five, who had probably just cried, or who would cry; and curled around her forehead, with just enough pressure to cause a line of folds in the skin above her eyes, were two black hands; obviously power and strength slept somewhere within them but at this moment they were infinitely gentle, describing with eight fingers that moment when a grip of iron weakens to a caress of love."

This play, inspired by a photograph, explores the nature of relationships between black men and white women.

For a free copy of our complete list
of plays and theatre books write to:
AMBER LANE PRESS
Church Street, Charlbury, Oxford OX7 3PR
Telephone and fax: 0608 810024